Big Kids Song Day

By Cameron Macintosh

T0360191

"It will be Big Kids Song Day
in six days," said Mr Kim.
"We will sing this song
for the mums and dads."

"This is such a fun song!"
I said.
"It will be a buzz
to sing it for them!"

"Can you sing this bit?"
Mr Kim said to Kang.

"Yes!" said Kang.

Kang sang it well!

It's Big Kids Song Day!

Mum, Dad, Nan and Pop
are here.

We are dressed up to sing.

Let's sing the song!

"Can you sing Kang's bit, Ash?" said Mr Kim.

"I will sing it as well as I can," I said.

I sang Kang's bit
of the song.

It was such a big buzz!

"Well sung, Ash!"
said Pop and Nan.

"Ash rocks!" said Kang.

CHECKING FOR MEANING

1. What type of song were the children singing for the mums and dads? *(Literal)*

2. Why couldn't Kang sing on Big Kids Song Day? *(Literal)*

3. Which words tell you that Ash did a great job singing Kang's part in the song? *(Inferential)*

EXTENDING VOCABULARY

song	What is the short vowel sound in this word? Can you change this letter to make other words that have been used in the story?
sick	What are the sounds in this word? Can you take away the letter s and put another letter or letters at the start to make new words? E.g. kick, brick, thick.
rocks	There are several meanings of the word *rocks*. What are they? Can you use the word in different sentences to show its different meanings?

MOVING BEYOND THE TEXT

1. What types of songs do you like to sing?

2. Why do people dress up when they sing at a concert?

3. Do you think Ash is a good singer? Why?

4. What are some other reasons parents come to school to watch their children?

SPEED SOUNDS

| sh | ch | th | th | ck | ng |

voiced   unvoiced

PRACTICE WORDS

sing

Song

such

song

Kang

sick

sang

Ash

sung

rocks